Johannes Gutenberg

Betty Lou Kratoville

High Noon Books
Novato, California

Cover Design: Nanette Brichetto
Cover Photo: Pictorial History Research
Interior Illustrations: North Wind Picture Archives

International Standard Book Number: 1-57128-142-8

10 09 08 07 06 05 04 03
1   0   9   8   7   6   5   4   3

Contents

CHAPTER 1

Books in the 1300s

Pick a book. Any book. A book of stories. A book of poems. A dictionary. A cookbook. The Bible. Just suppose that every single letter, every single number in that book had to be copied by hand! And it had to be copied clearly so that other people could read it. How long do you think it would take? Who would do it? Would you?

Hard to believe but this is how the world once was. It did not matter that people like you and me were not taught to read, for there were no books. Or almost none.

Before the 1400s books had to be copied by hand. This dull, boring work was almost always done by monks. Monks were thoughtful men who gave their lives to the church. They could be found at prayer in chapels or tending herbs in their gardens. Some with nimble fingers spent their lives in hushed rooms. Here they copied page after page of the Bible. Did they never grow tired? Did their fingers never cramp? In today's fast-paced world it is hard to believe that such men lived and worked.

Would you like to try this? Take a book from a shelf. Find a page to copy. Use your best penmanship, for, as in the days of the monks, others will be reading your work. Now you have finished. Do you still take the printed pages in your books for granted – as we all do?

What happened to change this? A single man found a way to solve this problem. Today he is known as the father of modern printing.

Johannes Gutenberg was his name. (In English he would be called John Goodmountain.) We do not know exactly when he was born. Why not? Because, of course, no *printed* records could be kept in those days. Some families wrote down important dates in their Bibles if they were lucky enough to have one. And few did. A Gutenberg family Bible has never been found. So we can only make a rough guess. It is thought that his birth took place about 600 years ago in the late 1300s in the busy town of Mainz. It is also thought that he had one brother and one sister.

Johannes was lucky. He was born into a rich German family. His father held an important job. He was Master of the Mint in the town of Mainz.

Often, at the breakfast table young Johannes would ask, "Father, may I go to the Mint with you today?"

His father would take a bite of his warm oatcake and say, "Yes, my boy." He was pleased that his son wanted to know what went on at the Mint. And he knew that his workmen liked the boy. They did not mind his questions. These workmen were all skilled goldsmiths. It was their job to stamp letters and numbers on gold coins. Johannes never grew tired of watching them at their tasks. How clever they were! He hoped one day that he might be a goldsmith.

He also liked to visit the places where the town's monks lived and worked. These church houses were called monasteries. Here Johannes often stood for hours at the side of the patient monks. Dip, dip, dip went their pens and brushes. Hour after hour they copied Bible verses onto heavy parchment. A single copy might take years to complete. What if one were stolen? Disaster! One of the monks came up with a good idea. All of the rare hand-drawn works were chained to shelves!

Johannes did not envy these men. In fact, it may have been then that a seed was planted in his mind. There had to be an easier way to make books!

CHAPTER 2

The Apprentice

In the 1300s boys of rich families were taught at home. Johannes's mother was the daughter of a shopkeeper. She had learned to read, write, and do sums in her father's shop. She passed onto her young son all that she knew.

Years passed. Johannes was no longer a child. One day his father said, "How would you like to go to work for me?"

"Would I be an apprentice?" asked Johannes. He knew that it took years for an apprentice to learn a trade.

"Yes," said his father. "One day you will be a fine goldsmith."

"Thank you, Father. That is what I always wanted to do. When do I start?" asked Johannes.

"Tomorrow," answered Mr. Gutenberg.

The next day Johannes went to work at the Mint. He liked his work, and he did it well. Yet his mind wandered. He could not forget his friends the monks. He could not forget their strict demanding lives. He had never heard them complain. Yet he felt there must be something that he could do.

What about the stamping craft of the goldsmiths? Was there any way it could be used to fit the needs of the monks? Probably not. Yet one thought after another kept floating through his head.

At this time France and England had been at war on and off for years. It had gone on so long it was called the Hundred Years' War. The constant fighting caused unrest all over Europe. One day riots broke out in Mainz. The richest citizens seemed most in danger. Mr. Gutenberg grew alarmed. Mainz was no longer a safe place to live. The Gutenberg family left Mainz in a rush. They fled to the peaceful town of Strasbourg. They had to leave most of their fortune behind.

Now hard times fell on the family. Johannes started to look for a job – any job. At last he found one. It paid little but it helped. Each day he sat at a long table with a group of men. They spent long hours cutting and polishing stones. Other workers took the stones and made them into cheap jewelry. During these dreary days Johannes did not forget his early daydreams about making books.

He would stumble on an idea. Yes! That might work. Then later – no, it wouldn't. Another day, a new thought. No, not good enough. Then another brainstorm – well perhaps this one held the answer.

The years were passing. He was getting older. He had to do *something*. At first he had only a knife and a few chunks of wood. He carved the 26 letters of the alphabet backwards on 26 small blocks of wood. He bored a tiny hole through the side of each block. Then he strung the blocks together. Next, he dipped the string of blocks into black ink. He used his full weight to press the blocks onto a piece of paper. Rough, yes, but it was a beginning.

Then one day a workable idea began to form in his mind. Pieces of metal type could be moved from place to place. Might this be the answer? He had to try!

To put his plan into action, Johannes needed money. He had none of his own. What to do? He went to friends and family. At last he found three men who agreed to become his partners. He made an amazing request of these men. He wanted them to invest their money – as much and as soon as possible. But he didn't want to tell them what he was working on. He was afraid that his strange ideas might cause them to change their minds. Oddly enough, they agreed to his terms.

Of course, this kind of work was hard to keep secret. One day his partners found out what he was doing. Were they angry? They were not! The idea sounded so good that they gave him more money. Now Gutenberg was able to buy a supply of lead. With this he could start to build some sort of printing machine. He also began to make single letters from lead. It was slow work. There were days when he almost gave up. Surely

The First Printing Press

there were other things in life. Things that were fun. Things that might make him rich. Then he would remember the monks in their small dark rooms and go back to work.

On Christmas Day one of his partners died. This man had two brothers who wanted to take his place in the company. For some reason Gutenberg did not trust them. "Never!" he thundered. They took him to court. The case was a short one. Gutenberg won it and went back to his cluttered workbench.

After a short time the other two partners lost interest and vanished. Now Gutenberg was in real trouble. He lived on small rents that came in from some family property in Mainz. But this simply was not enough. By 1342 he was out of money and supplies, and he dropped from sight. There is no record of how or where he spent the next few years.

CHAPTER 3

A Fresh Start

One day Gutenberg turned up in Mainz. His pockets were still empty. He went to a member of the family for help. This man lent Gutenberg a small sum of money. Hooray! He set up a new shop. His first attempts failed one after another. Yet he kept on trying. It was during this time that he thought of using metal sticks. Each stick would have a raised letter on its end – something like the letters on early typewriters.

Gutenberg had always loved the beauty of

the monks' handwritten books. So he made his letters look just like theirs. (This is why today his first books are still thought to be great works of art.)

It took months to cast all of the letters onto the ends of the metal sticks. Then he had to build a press to hold them. Now the time had come to put his methods to the test. He still had a bit of the loan left. He used the last of it to print a few copies of a well-known grammar book. Grammar had begun to be important to scholars in those days. A few people were happy to see Gutenberg's new grammar book. But it is hard to understand why some people still liked the old handmade books better.

Gutenberg kept trying new ways to use his molds and press. It seemed that at last he was on the road to success. Not so! His experiments ate up a lot of money. The press had to have special ink. The paper had to be of the finest quality. Costs for the lead that was needed to cast the type were high. After two years the entire loan had been used up.

Now an important man entered the life of Johannes Gutenberg. His name was Johann Fust. Old records are not clear about him. Some say he was a goldsmith. Others say he was a lawyer. But all agree that he had a great deal of money.

Was Fust a friend or foe? At first it seemed as if he were a friend. He was willing to invest his own money in Gutenberg's odd company. And we should give him a certain amount of credit. In those days not many people had faith in Gutenberg. Most Mainz citizens felt he had been wasting his time for years. A printing press to make books? Nonsense! Let the monks do it!

Fust seemed able to grasp what the printing of books in large quantities might mean to the world. There are those who think Fust cared more about what it would put in his own pocket! But at any rate Fust lent Gutenberg a large sum of money. Now Gutenberg was able to set up a better print shop. He could buy the supplies he needed. This was the start of Fust's place in the history of printing. It would go on for a long, long time.

Each man had his part to play in this plan. It was strictly business. Fust would put up the money. It was agreed that Gutenberg would pay it all back in two years. For his part, Gutenberg pledged everything he owned. This meant that if he could not repay the large loan when it came due, he would lose all of his equipment – *everything*! He was taking a huge risk. But what else could he do?

CHAPTER 4

Full Speed Ahead

Now it seemed as if nothing could stop Gutenberg. He needed a man to help him. He hired Peter Schoeffler. We do not know a lot about Peter Schoeffler. But we do know one important fact: As a child he had been adopted by Johann Fust!

His foster father had made sure that Schoeffler got a good education. We know that Peter brought a number of skills to his work with Gutenberg. His handwriting was very clear. So he often worked as a scribe. He knew quite a lot about the goldsmith's trade. But whether or not he was honest and loyal to his boss, Gutenberg, is still not known. One thing is clear. Gutenberg was pleased to have this hard-working young man at his side.

The two men chose the Bible as their first big undertaking. What a job it was! Just setting the type took three years. Each sheet of paper had to be cut to the right size by hand. After one side was printed, the sheet had to be hung up to dry before the other side could be printed. Any slight blur meant the sheet had to be thrown away and done again. Gutenberg began with four presses. Later he had six.

Fust and Gutenberg

At this time all Bibles were printed in Latin. There is no proof that Gutenberg ever studied Latin. Yet it must be so. He set type in this difficult language. He proofread it. It may be that at some time in his life he learned Latin at a German college. But we can find no solid clue that he did. All we know is that the type he set in Latin was perfect. Also, Peter Schoeffler knew Latin. That would have been a great help to Gutenberg.

Gutenberg and Schoeffler printed about two hundred copies of the Bible. There were two columns of type on each page. Each column had 42 lines of type. These early Bibles were known forever after as "the 42 line Bibles."

Now the hundreds of loose printed sheets had to be bound. Whoever did the binding would need to know his trade well. Gutenberg chose the bookbinder Heinrich Cremer. It was a good choice.

Cremer bound 642 sheets into two volumes. First, sections had to be sewn together by hand. Then, they were put between boards. The boards were then bound in leather. The bookbinder also had to add certain touches of color and design. All in all, the binding job took between six and nine months.

It should have been the moment for which Gutenberg had worked and waited. It was not! Trouble came when he did not expect it. And from someone Gutenberg thought was a good friend.

Who had stayed in the background while the Bibles were printed? Who knew that it was time for Gutenberg to repay his loan? Who stood by quietly and bided his time? Enter Johann Fust!

CHAPTER 5

Takeover!

It is time we learned a bit more about Johann Fust. We know that he was a rich man. He made most of his wealth as a salesman. He traveled to college towns all over Germany. He sold manuscripts. This meant he knew the value of the printed word. This, of course, led to his interest in the art of printing.

Fust took care to tell his customers all about the new process. He told them that books printed on a press were bound to be much cheaper than handwritten texts. He could see that there was a strong interest in the new printed books. It seemed time to make his move.

Not once, but twice Fust had lent Gutenberg 800 gulden. (A gulden was then worth about forty cents.) For a while the two men had made a good fit. Gutenberg had worked hard at his new method. Fust had stayed in the background.

Then one day Fust heard that Gutenberg had almost finished 200 Bibles. We wonder could it have been Peter Schoeffler, his foster son, who gave him this news? At any rate, he went to see Gutenberg at once.

"The loan is due," he said.

Gutenberg was shocked! "I cannot pay you

at this time. The Bibles have not yet been sold," he said.

"No matter," replied Fust. "You owe me 2026 gulden."

Gutenberg stared at him. "2026 gulden? You lent me only 1600."

Fust was calm. "My dear fellow, you have forgot the interest on the loan."

Gutenberg could not believe his ears. "Interest? What interest? You told me there would be no interest."

Fust looked him straight in the eye. "Why would I lend money without interest? Here is your bill."

He handed Gutenberg a piece of paper. On it

was written:

1. First capital advance	=	800 gulden
2. 6% interest on same	=	250 gulden
3. Second capital advance	=	800 gulden
4. Interest on the foregoing	=	140 gulden
5. Compound interest	=	36 gulden
Grand total of the debt		2026 gulden

Gutenberg read the bill. He crumpled the piece of paper into a ball and threw it on the floor. "There is no way I will pay you this amount," he shouted.

Fust stooped over and picked up the bill. "We will let the courts settle this," he said. He stormed out of the shop where Peter Schoeffler and others were working.

The trial was a long one. The mayor and the city treasurer were the judges. Did either of them recognize the importance of what Gutenberg had done? It is clear that they did not. Gutenberg lost the case.

Since that time most people have felt that the verdict was not fair. At the very least the court could have ordered that Gutenberg and Fust split the business and the 200 Bibles. But Fust was well-known and rich. Gutenberg was thought to be a little odd. What a strange fellow! Always messing about with ink and bits of paper.

The court ordered him to repay the loan at once. Of course, he could not do so. Fust wasted no time. He took charge of the printing shop. The first thing he did was to make Peter Schoeffler a full partner! A short time later Schoeffler married Fust's daughter. Now Gutenberg's employee had become Fust's son-in-law and half owner of the business!

Fust and Schoeffler set to work and finished the Bibles. They sold like hot cakes!

CHAPTER 6

Beginning Once Again

Did Gutenberg give up? Not the Johannes Gutenberg whose life we have been following! He began at once to search for a new sponsor. Many months went by. One day he bumped into an old friend on a Mainz street.

"Good morning," said his friend. "How are things going for you?"

"They could be better," replied Gutenberg. He was looking a bit shabby and downcast.

His friend clapped him on his shoulder.

"What's the matter, old friend?"

"It's that devil Fust," said Gutenberg. "He and Schoeffler have sold all of my Bibles. Now he is richer than ever. And my pockets are still empty."

"You need a new sponsor, Johannes. Then you could print more Bibles. Bibles that would be better than the ones Fust is selling," said the friend.

Gutenberg gave a sad smile. "But where can I find a sponsor? I've been looking for months. No one wants to help me. They just laugh and say I should try another line of work."

"What about Dr. Konrad Hemery?" asked the friend. "Do you know him? He's a very rich man

man and known for his kindness."

"I have heard his name. But I have never met him," said Gutenberg.

"Well, you should," said his friend. "Hemery is an honest man. You can trust him. Everyone in Mainz thinks highly of him. Once he and some other citizens learned the whole Mainz town council was dishonest. He forced them all to resign. He took over as town clerk. Since then, things have been much better in Mainz. I would be glad to see that you meet him. Then it will be up to you, Johannes. You will have to make him believe that your ideas will work."

"Please set up a meeting. And it should be just as soon as possible," said Gutenberg. Now he was smiling.

The friend was true to his word. A time and place for Gutenberg and Dr. Hemery to meet was quickly set. The meeting went well. The two men liked one another at once. The terms they agreed on were the same as those Gutenberg once had with Fust. Yet not the same. Hemery had enough money. He didn't need any more. He simply wanted Gutenberg to succeed. Why? Because he knew how important it was that word about the art of printing was spread.

It is clear that Gutenberg wanted this, too. He had stood by and watched Fust and Schoeffler quickly sell all the Bibles. He knew he had reason to be proud of the part he had played. But there was something else. It was more important. He worried about Fust and Schoeffler. He did not want them to keep the printing process from the world. He, too, had wished to keep his work a secret at one time. But no longer! He knew word of the Gutenberg Bibles had begun to spread. He knew that many men wanted to know about the new printing process. Gutenberg started sharing his methods with anyone who asked about them. This was one way of getting back at Fust and Schoeffler!

He also spent time making new type molds and building new presses. Better type. Better presses. He printed a new Bible. This Bible had 32 lines to a page. It became almost as well-known as the first 42-line Bible.

His best known work at this time was the *Catholicon*. The *Catholicon* was a huge Latin dictionary. It also served as an encyclopedia. That work took him three years. And no wonder! The text ran 744 pages. Gutenberg used a much smaller type for this work than that found in his 42-line Bible. Dr. Hemery gladly paid for this project. He was well rewarded. The *Catholicon* was a best-seller almost at once.

About this time Gutenberg also printed a calendar. It showed the phases of the moon and much more about the skies. People gathered on street corners in Mainz to admire the latest product of Gutenberg's lively brain. These same

Page from the 42-line Bible

39

people were puzzled by Gutenberg. The Bible, the *Catholicon*, and the calendar did not bear his name. In fact, throughout his life he never signed any of his works. And people today are still wondering why.

CHAPTER 7

Books Galore

Before Gutenberg, the number of handwritten books in Europe could be counted in the thousands. By 1500, after only 50 years of printing, there were more than nine million books!

Gutenberg died in 1468. His last years were calm and free from trouble. He was granted a pension by the archbishop of Mainz, Archbishop Adolph. A letter from the archbishop told the terms of the pension Gutenberg would receive each year:

1. Clothes (like that of a nobleman)

2. Wine for household use

3. Grain to last a year

Also, Gutenberg would not have to serve in the army. This seems odd, for by this time Gutenberg was in his sixties. Another ruling made better sense. Gutenberg would have to pay no taxes as long as he was "faithful and loyal" to the archbishop. This was a way to give honor in public to the inventor of book printing. And it most likely was a good move for Archbishop Adolph. He knew that powerful men in Rome had taken an interest in book printing. It would serve him well if he were kind to the man who had put books within reach of all.

During the years that followed, many men tried to take credit for Gutenberg's work. One of these was Johann Schoeffler. He was the son of Peter Schoeffler and the grandson of Johann Fust. He claimed that his father and grandfather were the real inventors. Then in 1505 he seems to have changed his mine. He wrote, "The art of typography was invented in 1450 by Johannes Gutenberg."

Today Johann Schoeffler, Peter Schoeffler, and Johann Fust are forgotten. The name of Johannes Gutenberg is honored everywhere. Only a few copies of his first printing have survived. They are thought of as priceless treasures and are guarded carefully.

We all owe a huge debt to this stubborn genius who would not give up, who brought light into a dark world.